Usborne Flip-Flap

How are babies made?

Alastair Smith

Illustrated by Maria Wheatley

Designed by Ruth Russell

Digital artwork by Fiona Johnson

Series editor: Judy Tatchell

There's a baby in there

All babies start inside their mothers. They grow and grow until they're big enough to live in the world outside.

New babies

Even newborn babies look different from each other.

Some are big...

Some have lots of hair...

...Some have none at all.

...Some are small.

But all babies are made in the same way. This book will tell you how.

Where does the baby grow?

The baby grows in a part of the body called the womb. Only girls and women have a womb.

The girl is pointing to where the womb is.

Safe and sound

The baby has everything it needs inside its mother's womb. It is safe and warm. It grows there until it is ready to come out into the world.

How long does the baby stay inside the mother?

Look how quickly the baby grows!

This is the baby after just six weeks.

This will be the head.

This will be an eye.

This is the tube that carries food and drink from the mother.

This is the baby's real size.

Baby's getting big

The baby grows and grows inside the mother's womb. The womb is like a tough sack full of watery liquid.

Starting to show

After about four months, the baby starts to make a bump in its mother's tummy.

Some of the time, the baby is awake. But most of the time it sleeps.

When the mother walks around, the baby might be rocked to sleep.

When the mother is still, the baby might wake up. It starts to move around.

What does the baby do?

It does some of the things that you do.

Thumb sucking.

Hiccuping.

Peeing when it needs to.

But the baby never makes a noise.

Want to see the baby grow some more?

I've been growing for four months.

Even bigger

The baby keeps getting bigger and bigger. It is heavy for the mother to carry inside her.

Seeing

The baby's eyes work now. When it's awake, it opens its eyes. It can see colors and light coming in through its mother's skin.

This baby might see a warm red glow from the sun.

Hearing

The baby's ears work. It hears things that happen inside its mother.

The baby can hear its mother's heart beating.

gurgle gurgle

The baby can hear noises from its mother's stomach too.

chatter chatter

The baby can also hear things from outside.

Lungs for breathing

When the baby is born, it will have to breathe air, like you do. You use your lungs to breathe.

This is where your lungs are.

The baby on the flap has been inside for about seven months.

Will the baby get any bigger?

The baby is ready

It is time for the baby to come out. The mother's womb starts to squeeze. It is pushing the baby out.

Helping the mother

A nurse and a doctor look after the mother while she has her baby.

Nurse

Hard work

Getting the baby out can take hours. It makes the mother tired.

The baby squeezes out of the opening between the mother's legs.

What happens next?

The baby is born!!

What is it like for the baby?

Getting out is a tight squeeze for the baby.

The baby comes out from a place that is warm and cozy. Outside, it is brighter. Things are more lively and noisy.

The baby finds things strange.

What does the baby do as soon as it is out?

The new baby

The baby has been born. Now it does lots of new things. But first of all it is cuddled by its mother.

What the baby does

The baby has milk for its food. The milk comes from its mother's breasts.

Mothers only make milk when they have a baby.

Some mothers feed their babies with milk from a bottle.

The baby has to wear diapers to stop its pee and poop from making a mess.

Naming the baby

The mother and father choose a name for the baby.

Chris?... Jan?... Jamie?... Ali?... Frankie?...

Robin?... Jo?... Stevie?... Jamie?...

14

Other things to do

The baby looks around. It can only see things very close to it. Things far away look fuzzy.

The baby pushes its arms and legs in and out. It wiggles its body around.

What does the baby do most?

Index

Special thanks to Dr. Sarah Bower, Consultant in Fetal Medicine and Obstetrics at Harris Birthright Trust, London, for advice in the writing of this book.

First published in 1997 by Usborne Publishing Ltd, Usborne House, 83-85 Saffron Hill, London, EC1N 8RT, England. www.usborne.com Copyright © 2003, 1997 Usborne Publishing Ltd. First published in America 1998. AE.